KIDS
BOOK

KIDS BOOK

© Ms H5 2021

INTRODUCTION:

Author: Hazel Zitha

Designer & Author

BSc (Hons)Cognitive
Behavioural Therapy
(CBT)
Ms H5
Language: English

DESCRIPTION:

Kids Book © Ms H5 2021:
Home Learning activities & online
Virtual experience that is changing the
way we learn & do our research.
Schools are online supporting & having
the Zoom classes with students as well.
Bespoke online training with high
quality.
Professional development training
covering all Subjects & activities.
.Kids can access their online School
Libraries & other Libraries
& Learning Tools to improve.
Online Bookshelves are available 24/7
for kids to read &
learn more.
Benefits of online Learning classes can
be accessed at any
time over the Internet 24/7.

Kids who learn on virtual classrooms
have more opportunity
to meet, learn with other kids from
Other countries & backgrounds is a
good time to learn
about diversity.

Kids online learn Computer skills &
improve technical
skills as well.
To collaborate &
learn remotely can be a definite plus in
future good skills achievement.
Online Learning give kids the freedom
to learn at their own
pace with prerecorded virtual classes.
Kids can login & out when it's the best
time for them to
study & do their homework.
Kids learn to work as a team.
Education is a good tool that can
change the way we see
things & make a difference in the world.

February 06, 2021
Pages: 104

Prepared by:

© *M&H5* 2021

February 06, 2021
Pages: 104

KIDS BOOK

Prepared by:

© *M♦ H5* 2021

Chapter 1

MUM & DEE LEARNING FROM HOME

Mum & Dee...

Schools are closed and studying is done at home.
Dee continues education at home.
With Mum proper guidance.
Mum secure the necessary tools & resources.
Navigate them together.
Set up a routine.
Mum is also flexible.
Mum work at Dee's own pace.
Dee is allowed to take breaks in between.
All Toys are put away to minimize distractions.
Dee & Mum created a conducive learning environment & space.
Mum keep tabs on Dee's progress.

© *Ms H*5 2021

Chapter 1

MUM & DEE LEARNING FROM HOME
MUM & DEE...

Mum & Dee mix things up.

Mum & Dee try different activities to keep learning interesting.

Mum creates playful time and breaks.

Mum reminds Dee that, learning is fun.

Mum creates her own flexible structure.

Mum support & work with Teachers to deliver good education for Dee.

Mum always allow Dee to observe so she can learn from her as well.

Getting used to Learning from Home takes time & is different.

© *Ms H*5 2021

Candis is Smart ...

Chapter 2

CANDIS IS SMART

Candis...
Candis is going to answer all the following questions for us
Yes / No
True / False
Question 1
Our solar system has nine official planets.
Yes or No
Answer 1
In 2006, the International Astronomical Union changed
Pluto's designation from planet to a dwarf planet. This means
that instead of
nine, we only have eight true planets.
No
Question 2
All kittens are born with blue eyes.
True or False
Answer 2
All cats are born with blue eyes because their eyes don't
have melanin yet. This is the natural pigment that shows their eye
color. Their
melanocyte cells only start producing melanin at around 4 to 6
weeks, so that's
when their true eye color starts to show.
True

Chapter 2

CANDIS IS SMART CANDIS...

Multiple Choices

Question 3

What food is used to make the Mexican dish Guacamole?

a.   Zucchini

b.   Green Beans

c.   Avocado

d.   Chayote Squash

Answer 3

c. Avocado

Question 4

Fill in the Blanks

A shrimp's heart is located in its...?

Answer 4

A shrimp's heart is located in its...

Head

© Ms H5 2021

Chapter 2

CANDIS IS SMART CANDIS...

Question 5

Name the five great oceans of the world.

Answer 5

Pacific Ocean

Atlantic Ocean

Indian Ocean

Arctic Ocean

Southern Ocean

Question 6

The Cherry Blossom is the unofficial national flower of what country?

Answer 6

Japan

Well Done Candis...

© Ms H5 2021

Chapter 3

WILMA ACTIVITIES TO KEEP LEARNING FUN

Wilma...

Home learning shouldn't be all about the books. These activities can help.

Weekly craft projects

Wilma include tactile learning is a great way to learn by doing.

Art breaks

Wilma schedule is packed with creative breaks. They help recharge her mind.

Dad bring stories to life with he's voice & engage Wilma's imagination.

Encourage Quiet reading time as well

Allow Wilma to get lost in a good story.

Daily puzzle time

Dad prepare one challenge per day. It helps with problem solving

& teaches analytical skills.

Make learning fun

Search variety of home learning curriculum for a well rounded education check online & speak to the School Teachers as well for more information.

© *Ms H*5 2021

Robin Healthcare Tips...

© Ms H5 2021

Chapter 4

ROBIN HEALTHCARE TIPS

Robin...

Wash your hands.
Keeping yourself germs free.
Good hygiene means good health.
Dispose of tissue after use properly in the Bin.
Get more information from Parents & Teachers.
Remember good hygiene.
When you Cough or sneeze use a tissue.
Before you eat or handle food wash your hands.
Stay clean.
Stay safe.
Stay healthy is a shared duty.

© *Ms H5* 2021

Chapter 5

KIM DAILY MEAL PREP WHILE STUDYING FROM HOME

Kim...

Commit to eating well with these tips.
Talk with your family.
Know their favourite meals & dishes they are keen to try.
Research healthy recipes.
Intentionally insert dishes made with vegetables, fruits, & grains.
Make meal planning exciting.
Try out Meatless Mondays, Taco Thursdays or Fried Chicken.
Fridays so your family has food traditions to look forward to.
This makes meal planning easier to predict too.
Start small.
Whipping up dinners good for 3 to 4 days a week should be a
good place to begin meal prep at home.

© *Ms H*5 2021

Chapter 5

KIM DAILY MEAL PREP WHILE STUDYING FROM HOME
KIM...

Dedicate days in the week for meal prep.
Identify the day for planning the menu, shopping for
ingredients, and for cooking.
Stock up on staple ingredients.
Automate breakfast.
Overnight oats, cereals, fruits, and granola are no
stress
breakfast ideas you can incorporate on a daily basis.
Have enough containers.
Keep food by portion size while following proper
storage to
prevent spoilage.
The secret sauce of healthier food choices is in meal
planning.
Get into the habit!

© *Ms H5* 2021

Kids Book

Anton & the Love of Animals...

© Ms H5 2021

Chapter 6

ANTON & THE LOVE OF ANIMALS

Anton...

Yes or No
Multiple Choices
True or False
Fill in the Blanks
Question 1
The slowest animal in the world is a sloth.
Yes or No
Answer 1
Sloths move at a top speed of 0.003 miles per hour. Why they move ever so slow is to conserve the little energy they have in their bodies.
This is due to their highly herbivorous diet.
Yes

© *Ms H*5 2021

Chapter 6

ANTON & THE LOVE OF ANIMALS
ANTON...

Question 2
A group of lions is called a flock.
True or False
Answer 2
A group of lions is collectively called a pride.
For centuries, lions have been seen as noble & regal
creatures, hence their group name.
False
Question 3
The sleepiest animals on earth are snails. They can sleep
for how many years?
Answer 3
3 years
Question 4
Cats use their ...
to inspect if a space is too
small for them to fit through or not.
Answer 4
Cats use their... whiskers to
inspect if a space is too small for them to fit through or not.

Chapter 6

ANTON & THE LOVE OF ANIMALS
ANTON...

Question 5

Name 4 dog breeds that start with the letter G.

Answer 5

Golden Retriever

Great Pyrenees

German Shepherd

Great Dane

Question 6

Jellyfish are popular sea creatures from surface waters to the deep sea. They often move in groups. What do you call a group of jellyfish?

Answer 6

A bloom or a swarm.

Chapter 7

TEE BENEFITS OF FRUITS & MILK

Tee...

The importance of Nutrition
Healthy habit, you should try to eat more fruits each
day. Fruits are the best sources of fibre, vitamins,
minerals & antioxidants.
Pineapple
Rich in potassium, calcium, vitamin C, beta carotene,
thiamin, B6, as well as soluble & insoluble fiber.
Watermelon
Vitamin A, B1, B5, Magnesium
Orange
Oranges are an excellent source of vitamin C
Boosts immune system function
Thiamine, Vitamin B1
Folate
Potassium

© *Ms H*5 2021

Chapter 7

TEE BENEFITS OF FRUITS & MILK TEE...

Lemon

Lemons are an excellent source of vitamins such as vitamins B1,

B2, B6, potassium, calcium, magnesium & copper

Apple

Apples contain antioxidants, boasts vitamin K, fiber

Kiwi

Kiwis are also an excellent source of vitamin E, C, K, folate,

& potassium.

They also have antioxidants & are a good source of fiber.

Milk

Milk products have a good balance of proteins calcium.

Riboflavin, phosphorous, potassium, magnesium, zinc & Vitamins A, B12.

© *Ms H*5 2021

Eleanor Questions & Answer Time...

© Ms H5 2021

Chapter 8

ELEANOR QUESTIONS & ANSWER TIME

Eleanor...

Question 1

What is a Rose?

Answer 1

A rose is a woody perennial flowering plant of the genus Rosa, in the family Rosaceae or the flower it bears

Question 2

True or False

Global warming is a condition where there is an excess of carbon dioxide.

Answer 2

True

Carbon dioxide (CO_2) & other air pollutants can last for years in the atmosphere, trapping heat & causing the planet to get warmer.

© *Ms H*5 2021

Chapter 8

ELEANOR QUESTIONS & ANSWER TIME
ELEANOR...

Question 3

What's the difference between Principal and Principle?

Answer 3

Principal means primary or first.

Principle means a belief or a rule.

Question4

List the four main branches of science.

Answer 4

A. Math & Logic

B. Biological Science

C. Physical Science

D. Social Science

Filippa Daily Journal about Learning from Home...

© M. H 5 2 0 2 1

Chapter 9

FILIPPA
DAILY JOURNAL ABOUT   LEARNING FROM HOME

Filippa...

1.Set up your study space at home

Find an area in your home where you can sit
comfortably & focus.

Make it separate from a shared space.

Ideally away from a TV Room or other distractions.

2.Take down notes

Taking down notes & asking questions keeps your mind
engaged.

3. Plan your day ahead.

Always follow the schedule provided by your school, or
ask or one.

Write down your Study To Do List

Break down your list into small task starting with the
ones that

are the hardest first when you have energy.

© *Ms H*5 2021

Chapter 9

FILIPPA
DAILY JOURNAL ABOUT   LEARNING FROM HOME

Filippa...

4.Stay away from distractions.

Harness your imagination & follow instructions make
learning from home easy.

Put your phone away if you're doing your School
work.

Ask your parents for help if you're struggling don't be
afraid.

5.Take Breaks

In your To Do List add Breaks, to eat Breakfast,
Lunch, Snack,

water in between, take a walk for fresh air & stretch.

This will help you

recharge & relax.

6.Remember you're not alone ask for help & support
from School,

when things get hard.

Ask for help from your teachers & friends from
your class as well.

Support is available just ask.

© *M₃ H*5 2021

Chapter 9

FILIPPA
DAILY JOURNAL ABOUT LEARNING FROM HOME

Filippa...

7.Use My Daily Planner to write things you might
want to ask your teacher about the lessons later.
Use a Daily Journal to track your lesson progress &
time table.
Learning from home can be hard, but it's definitely
achievable.
Learning from Home does help reinforce important
skills, such
as time management, communication skills,
computer skills & more.

© *Ms H*5 2021

...Louis schedule for online virtual lessons at home...

© Ms H5 2021

Chapter 10

LOUIS SCHEDULE FOR ONLINE VIRTUAL LESSONS AT HOME

Louis...

Get properly dressed.
Look your best
& presentable.
Think of what you will wear make sure is comfortable.
Enjoy the fact that your classmates will be online with
you as well.
Stay in your comfortable chair.
Check if your systems are working, ask your parents
for help connecting.
Is your online Zoom app loading well?
Try bringing your computer or mobile device closer to
the WiFi router or access point at home.
Have your mobile data
internet ready in case your current connection is not
working.
Is your audio system working?
Find yourself a quiet spot at home to attend your class.

© *Ms H5* 2021

Chapter 10

LOUIS SCHEDULE FOR ONLINE VIRTUAL LESSONS
AT HOME
LOUIS...

Turn off the volume

of your TV or music player so you can focus.

Announce your arrival.

It's important to

hear your Teacher & classmates talk & that they hear

you clearly as well.

Set your Pen & Notepad ready.

Listen to your teacher & ask questions if you feel lost

or unclear.

Take your time.

Give your full attention.

Going from face to face class to online virtual class

can be a big change.

A supportive environment is key in helping everyone

transition to the new way of collaborating.

© Ms H5 2021

Chapter 11

ISABELLA FAVORITES MATHS SHAPES

Isabella...

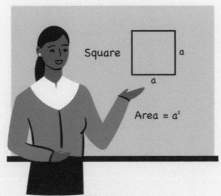

Circle
Triangle
Hexagon
Square-based pyramid
Cube
Square
Pentagon
Sphere
Triangular-based Pyramid
Triangular prism

© *Ms H5* 2021

Square

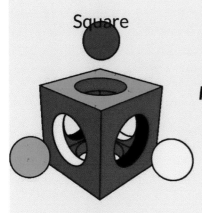

Chapter 11

ISABELLA FAVORITES MATHS SHAPES

Isabella...

Triangle

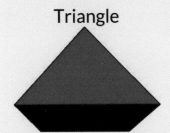

Circle

Hexagon

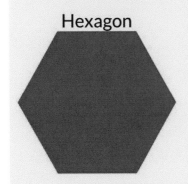

© *M♪H*5 2021

Carey
Math's & Symbols...

© Ms Hs 2021

Chapter 12

CAREY
MATH'S & SYMBOLS

Carey...

1. 101 + 100 =

2. 200 + 400 =

3. 301 + 399 =

4. 206 + 104 =

5. 199 + 401 =

6. 666 + 440 =

7. 719 + 521 =

8. 180 + 220 =

9. 982 + 188 =

10. 111 + 555 =

© *Ms H5* 2021

Chapter 12

CAREY
MATH'S & SYMBOLS

Carey...

OHM SIGN

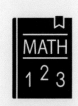

PLUS	**NOT EQUAL TO**	**RULER & PENCIL**

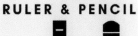

DIVIDED BY

MULTIPLIED BY

NOTE BOOK

SUM OF

EQUAL TO

COMPAS
SET SQUARE

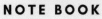

PI CONSTANT

SQUARE ROOT OF

CALCULATOR
& DOLLAR COIN

PERECENT

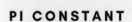

MINUS

© *Ms H*5 2021

Chapter 13

KAY FISHES NAMES LIST

Kay...
Shark
Whale
Starfish
Clownfish
Tuna
Goldfish
Eel
Delphine
Angelfish
Catfish
Oscar fish
Jelly fish
Stingray
Siamese fighting fish
Guppy fish
Puffer fish
Koi fish

© *M♪ H*5 2021

Chapter 13

KAY FISHES NAMES LIST

Kay...

Chapter 14

JENNY HEALTHY FOOD

Jenny...

Eggs
Hamburger
Milk
Cheese
Butter
Yoghurt
Pizza
Bacon
Salad bowl
Bread
Chicken
Donut

Chapter 14

JENNY HEALTHY FOOD

Jenny...

Tom word spelling...

© Ms H 5 2 0 2 1

Chapter 15

TOM WORD SPELLING

Tom...
School
Train
Truck
Boat
Ruler
Book
Journal
Computer
Pen
Glue
School Bus
Racecar
Crayons
Chalkboard
Scissors
School bus
Boat
Motorcycle
Dump truck

© *Ms H* 5 2021

Chapter 15

TOM WORD SPELLING

Tom...

© Ms H5 2021

Tatianna Summer exciting activities...

© M s H 5 2 0 2 1

Chapter 16

TATIANNA SUMMER EXCITING ACTIVITIES

Tatianna...
Summer Holiday
Lego Play
Football Camps
Flip flop
Ice cream
Pool
Umbrella
Sand
Shell
Beach
Popsicle
Soda
Ice cream
Sand bucket
Tent
Beach hut
Sunscreen
Hat
Sunglasses
Water
Vacation
Picnic
Sunshine

© *Ms H5* 2021

Chapter 16

TATIANNA SUMMER EXCITING ACTIVITIES

Tatianna...

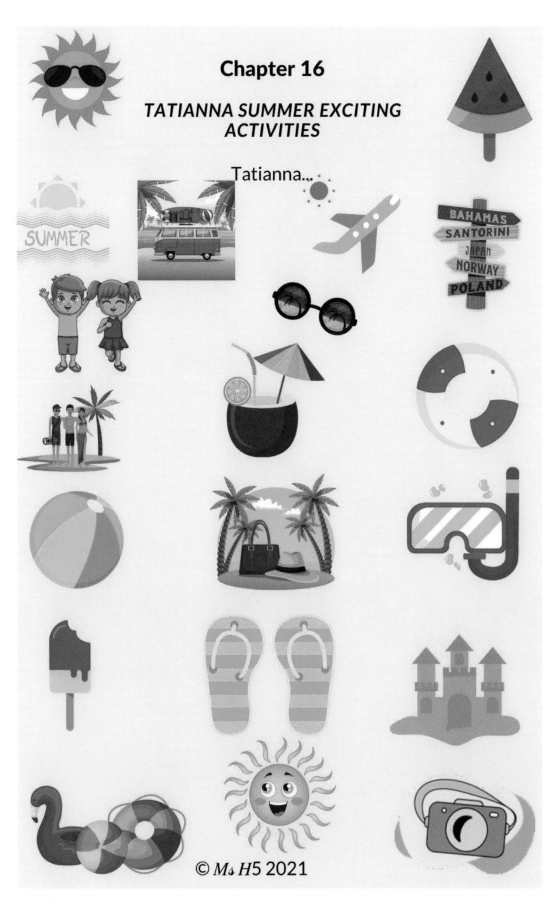

© *Ms H5* 2021

Charles Mental Health Check In...

© M♂ H5 2O2I

Chapter 17

CHARLES MENTAL HEALTH CHECK IN

Charles...
1. Sad

2. Unhappy

3. Calm

4. Happy

5. Motivated

© *Ms H*5 2021

Chapter 17

CHARLES MENTAL HEALTH CHECK IN

Charles...
Mental Health Check In

1. I feel OK

2. I'm getting there

3. Having a hard time

4. Pretty good

5. I need support

© *M♪ H5* 2021

Marvin
Science Lab Tools ...

Chapter 18

MARVIN
SCIENCE LAB TOOLS ...

Science Lab Tools
Erlenmeyer flask
Test Tube rack
Beaker
Test Tube
Alcohol burner
Pipette
Conical Flask
Microscope & more...

Chapter 18

MARVIN
SCIENCE LAB TOOLS

Marvin...

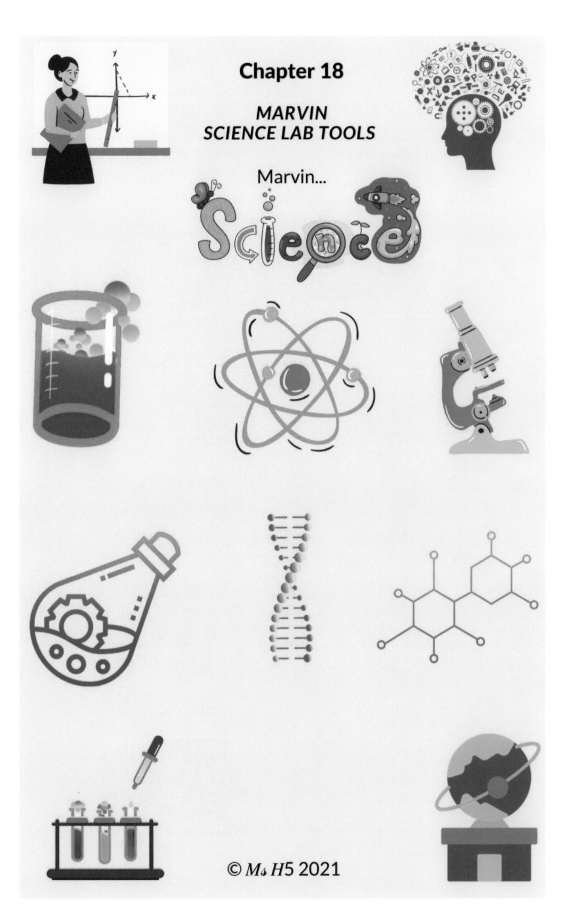

Chapter 18

MARVIN SCIENCE LAB TOOLS

Marvin…

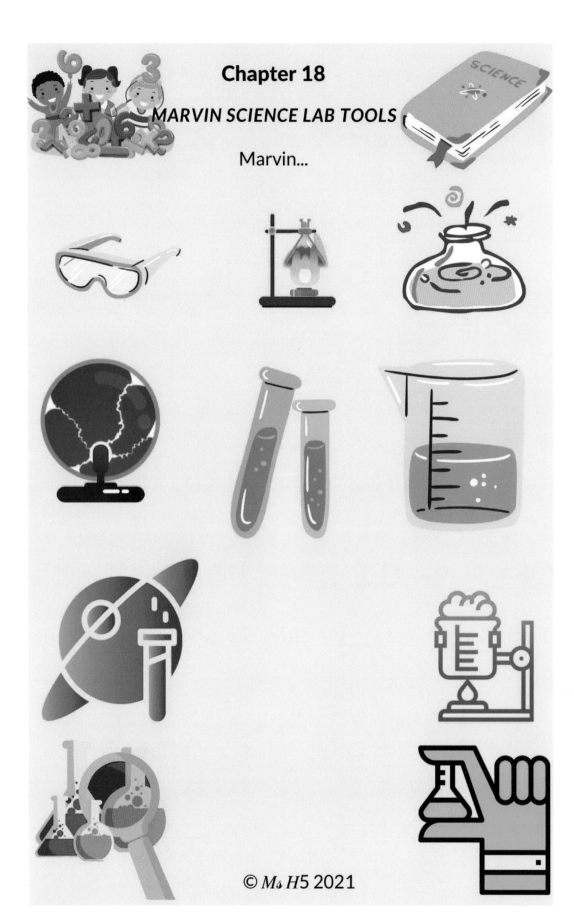

Chapter 19

ROBERT WEATHER FORECAST

Robert...

Rain
Clouds
Rainbow
Showers
Snow
Moon
Windy
Storm
Hot
Cold
Thunderstorm
Tornado
Lightning
Clear

© *Ms H5* 2021

Chapter 19

ROBERT WEATHER FORECAST

Robert...

© *M♪ H*5 2021

Rod Yoga Class...

Chapter 20

ROD
YOGA CLASS

Rod...

Rod Pose
Prayer Pose
Tree Pose
Raised Hands Pose
Chair Pose
Lunge Pose
Warrior Pose
Take a break for few minutes
Start again
Few steps
Small steps to relax & keep active...

© *Ms H5* 2021

Chapter 20

ROD
YOGA CLASS

Rod...

Chapter 21

NINA CLIPART

Nina...

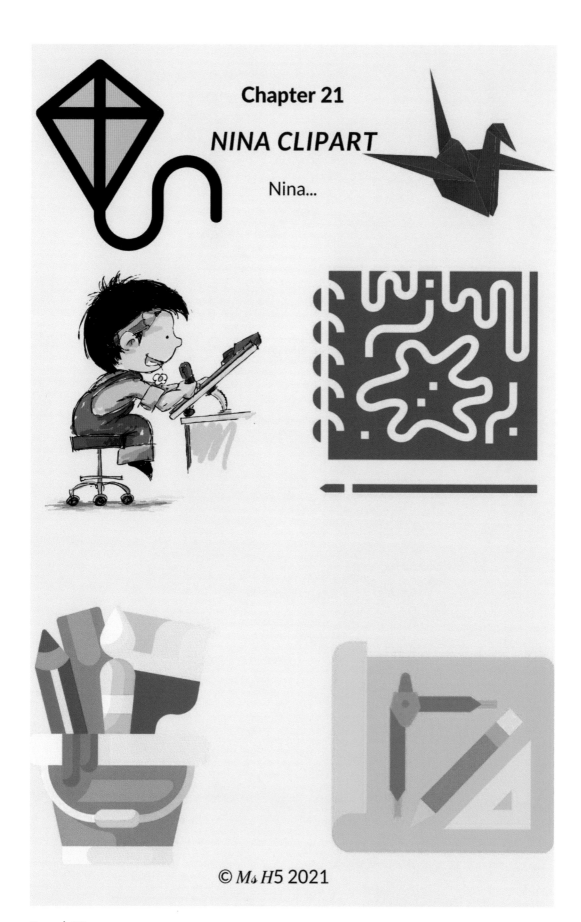

Chapter 22

Ms H LEARNING CENTRE

Ms H Learning Centre...

© Ms H5 2021

Chapter 23

NICOLAS BRAINSTORM

Nicolas...

Draw a story map
Write out goals in each category
Colour my story map
1. Family: help to set up the dinner table on time.
2. Friends: chat on a group chat 2 x a week.
3. School: Ask for more support in Math's class.
4. Rugby: Thursday.
5.Boxing:Tuesday.
6. Art Class: Improve to get higher grades.

Chapter 23

NICOLAS BRAINSTORM

Nicolas...

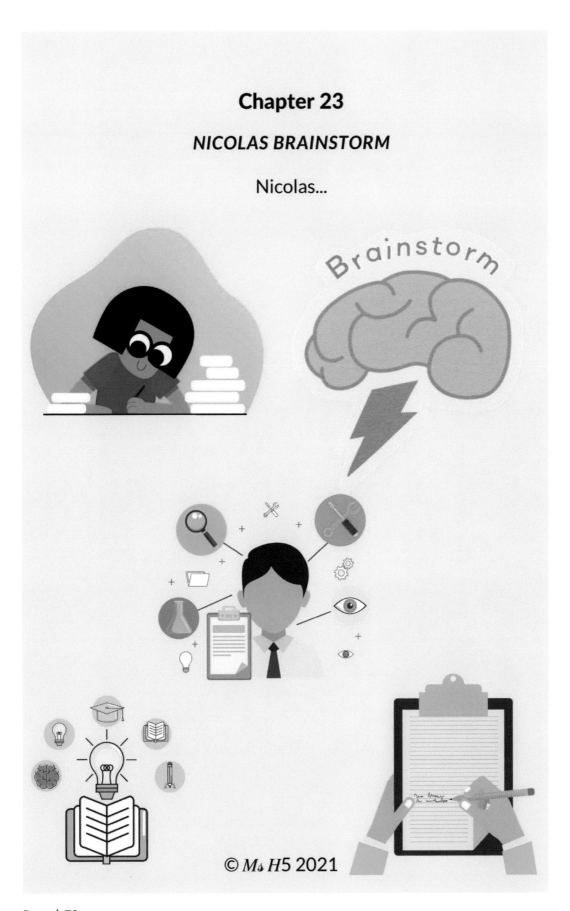

Chapter 24

M♭H ONLINE BOOKSHELVES

M♭H Online...
eBooks
Kindle Unlimited
Paperback Books
Enjoy the freedom to Explore eBooks &
other online Books to read.
Read anywhere & anytime online.
Regular reading improves brain connectivity
& increases your vocabulary.
Reading triggers creativity, vivifying the
imagination in children.
Learning from our mistakes help us
improves.
Education is good for children remember we
learn through making mistakes...

Chapter 24

Ms H ONLINE BOOKSHELVES

Ms H Online...

Trudy
& Etta time for animal knowledge...

Chapter 25

TRUDY
& ETTA TIME FOR ANIMAL KNOWLEDGE

Trudy & Etta...

Question 1

What food makes up nearly all around 99% of a Giant

Panda's diet?

Answer 1

Bamboo

Question 2

What is the only continent on earth where Giraffes

live in the wild?

Answer 2

Africa

Question 3

Bees

are found on every continent of earth except for one,

which is it?

Answer 3

Antarctica

Question 4

Is a shark a fish or a mammal?

Answer 4

A Fish

Question 5

How many legs does a spider have?

Answer 5

8

© *M♪H*5 2021

Chapter 25

TRUDY
& ETTA TIME FOR ANIMAL KNOWLEDGE

Trudy & Etta...

© M♪ H5 2021

Edward is learning more about the environment....

© M H 5 2 0 2 1

Chapter 26

EDWARD IS LEARNING MORE ABOUT THE ENVIRONMENT

Edward...
Edward is learning more about the environment, recycling,
animals & plants

Question 1

What are the 3 R's of recycling?

Answer 1

Reduce, reuse & recycle.

Question 2

What state of the USA is the Grand Canyon located in?

Answer 2

Arizona

Question 3

True or false?

Burning or logging naturally occurring forests is known as
deforestation.

Answer 3

True

Question 4

True or false?

Earth Day is held on June 18.

Answer 4

False (April 22)

Question 5

Avers Rock in Australia is also known as what?

Answer 5

Uluru

© Ms H5 2021

Lily learning about plants...

© M♪ H5 2 0 2 1

Chapter 27

LILY LEARNING ABOUT PLANTS

Lily...

Question 1

What grain has the highest level of worldwide production?

Answer 2

Maize

Question 2

The Japanese word sakura means the blossoming of what kind of tree?

Answer 2

Cherry tree

Question 3

The scientific study of plant life is known as what?

Answer 3

Botany

Question 4

True or false?

Humans were on Earth before plants.

Answer 4

False

Question 5

The process of plants using energy from sunlight to turn carbon dioxide into food is known as what?

Answer 5

Photosynthesis

© *Ms H* 5 2021

Arlen & Tasha Space activities...

© Ms H5 2021

Chapter 28

ARLEN & TASHA SPACE ACTIVITIES

Arlen & Tasha...

Question 1

Is the sun a star or a planet?

Answer 1

A star

Question 2

What

is the name of the force holding us to the Earth?

Answer 2

Gravity

Question 3

What is the closest planet to the Sun?

Answer 3

Mercury

Question 4

What planet is famous for its big red spot on it?

Answer 4

Jupiter

Question 5

What planet is known as the red planet?

Answer 5

Mars

Gareth put Dinosaur knowledge to the test...

© M S H 5 2 O 2 I

Chapter 29

GARETH PUT DINOSAUR KNOWLEDGE TO THE TEST

Gareth...

Question 1

True or false?

The name dinosaur means terrible lizard.

Answer 1

True

Question 2

Apatosaurus is also widely known by what other name?

Answer 2

Brontosaurus

Question 3

Which came first, the Jurassic or Triassic Period?

Answer 3

The Triassic Period

Question 4

A person who studies fossils & prehistoric life such as dinosaurs is known as a what?

Answer 4

Paleontologist

Question 5

True or false?

Birds evolved from dinosaurs.

Answer 5

True

© *Ms H*5 2021

Chapter 29

GARETH PUT DINOSAUR KNOWLEDGE TO THE TEST

Gareth...

Vaughntest your knowledge of the world

Countries...

abc

© M ♪ H 5 2 0 2 1

Chapter 30

VAUGHN TEST YOUR KNOWLEDGE OF THE WORLD COUNTRIES

Vaughn...

Question 1

In what country would you find the cities Glasgow and Edinburgh?

Answer 1

Scotland

Question 2

In what country was Nelson Mandela born?

Answer 2

South Africa

Question 3

What country was the first to land a man on the moon?

Answer 3

USA

Question 4

In what country is the Great Pyramid of Giza found?

Answer 4

Egypt

Question 5

Mount Fuji is the highest mountain in what country?

Answer 5

Japan

Easter tradition & feast...

Chapter 31

EASTER TRADITION & FEAST

Easter Treats...

Easter marks the beginning of spring.
Decorate your Easter basket.
Hide some Easter Eggs for Easter eggs Hunt.
Prepare some Easter treats to share with
friends & family.
Starts with a basket filled to the brim of hot
cross bun, Easter
eggs, bunnies, Carrot cake, Macarons,
Cupcakes, Pancakes Marshmallow, Doughnuts
& lots of Treats.
You'll have to be serving Easter treats all day
long.
Easter treats with a good dinner.
Easter Bunny Juice, Easter Punch, Easter
Mocktail.
Don't forget to take beautiful pictures to share
with your
classmates & friends.

© *Ms H*5 2021

Chapter 31

EASTER TRADITION & FEAST

Easter Treats...

© M♪H5 2021

Chapter 32

LET'S PLAY A HALLOWEEN GAME

Halloween...
Whoever answers the most questions correct wins the game.
The winners will get a special prize.
Show off your Halloween knowledge.
Question 1
What is the number one city for trick or treating in the United States?
Answer 1
San Francisco
Question 2
Apart from sucking human blood, what do vampires and bats
have in common?
Answer 2
They only come out at night.
Question 3
True or false
The word 'hallow' means saint or holy person?
Answer 3
True
Question 4
What date is Halloween celebrated?
Answer 4
October 31st
Question 5
Instead of candy, what did kids originally receive when trick or treating?
Answer 5
Food & drinks

Chapter 32

LET'S PLAY A HALLOWEEN GAME

Halloween...

HAPPY HALLOWEEN

TRICK OR TREAT

SPOOKY

ZOMBIE

© Ms H5 2021

How to Build a Snowman...

© Ms H5 2021

Chapter 33

HOW
TO BUILD A SNOWMAN
SNOWMAN...

Follow the instructions...
1. Find two sticks for arms.
2. Gather a patch of snow & begin to roll it into a ball. Make sure you squeeze the snow together so that it is tightly stuck together.
3. When your done with the body make the head.
4. Find a carrot for a sharp nose.
5. Find 3 stones for snowman's eyes & mouth.
6. Dress your snowman in a hat & scarf.
7. Remember when the weather get warm the snowman will melt!

Chapter 33

HOW
TO BUILD A SNOWMAN
SNOWMAN...

Follow the instructions...

Chapter 34

SANTA
CLAUS ANSWER! QUESTIONS
ABOUT CHRISTMAS

Santa Claus...

Question 1

What was the first company that used Santa Claus
in advertising?

Answer: 1

Coca-Cola

Question 2

Which popular Christmas beverage is also called
milk punch?

Answer 2

Eggnog

Question 3

Which country did eggnog come from?

Answer 3

England

Question 4

Where was baby Jesus born?

Answer 4

In Bethlehem

Question5

What words follow Silent Night in the song?

Answer 5

Holy night

Chapter 34

SANTA CLAUS ANSWER! QUESTIONS ABOUT CHRISTMAS

Santa Claus...

© Ms H5 2021

Kids Book

Ms H5 Art &Crafts ideas...

© *Ms H* 5 2 0 2 1

Chapter 35

Ms H5 ART & CRAFTS IDEAS

Ms H5...

Printed in Great Britain
by Amazon